For Pa

And with thanks to Nigel, all my friends in the Norwich Poetry Group for their help and encouragement, and to Aude for her generous support.

The Sumerian Myth

The original Sumerian story of Inanna's descent to the underworld dates from 2,000 B.C. It tells how Inanna, queen of Heaven and consort of Dumuzi, the shepherd king, decides to visit her sister Ereshkigal, queen of the underworld.

Ereshkigal decrees that Inanna's regalia be removed piece by piece as she passes through the seven gates and when her denuded sister enters her presence, she looks on her with her eyes of death and hangs her corpse on a meat-hook.

When, after three days, Inanna fails to return to the surface, the god Enki creates from the dirt beneath his fingernails, two little creatures, the kurgarra and the galatur, who enter the underworld and, by showing sympathy with Ereshkigal, win the body of Inanna. They sprinkle it with the bread and water of life so Inanna revives and is able to return to the surface.

This story is still richly symbolic and meaningful for our time, and in this book I have retold the tale in a modern setting, reflected on it, and, using the prerogative of the story-teller, continued it.

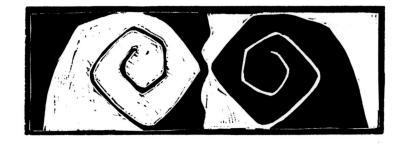

Autumn Journey

I drive by pale, shadowed stubble-fields
and, like a memory, your skin, Inanna,
though so faint, so faint.
Measurably clear in the bright desert,
blazing and fixed above the ziggurats,
and here so lost, so vague,
as imperceptible as mist in this autumn evening.

Unblinkered, unforgiving, steely, the cars.
Their speed, their noise, by destroying inattention,
wipe out your voice.
Where mules and camels plodded timelessly,
loud over the whole caravan, your song,
unwavering, strong,
celebrated, interpreted the journey.

Here traffic passes, junctions, converges,
office blocks scatter your sky, so I
neither hear you nor see you.
How superimpose on this mapped, computerised,
squared-up, bright, blind city
a crumbling chart
old sand-blocked paths and half-lost hieroglyphs?

But though outbeamed, dislocated, outsped,
and like old tablets blurred, Inanna,
surely not dead, not dead.
Won't you smash for me the strictures of the city,
orientate me to your indriven direction,
guide me, teach me to see
your softer light and different clarity?

Ereshkigal Demands

No, not Inanna, not her!
Don't cry to her, don't!
Look downwards instead.
Turn your head to the ground.
Examine the canyons, the bedrock.
Take note of me, Ereshkigal.

My force could flare into life,
but you have locked me in hell,
imprisoned me, called me evil,
treated me as dead matter
to be hacked, rammed with machinery,
manipulated how you will.

Fools! Turn lightward all you may,
I'm here, and I'm rampant anger,
planning to burst like a boil,
poison your rivers, your rain,
cover your soil with pus,
encrust your sweet seas with oil.

Averting your eyes from the hurt, are you?
Just bend and inspect the sore!
If you pull apart the lips of the wound,
you'll see how infection swarms!
I am clogged with fermenting energy,
turn to me, turn to me urgently!

Daylight

Above the city now, still scanning the sky
for you, Inanna,
Your dark sister's stark anger I heard clearly—
the earth is still cringing –
but the difficulty is to spy you, the bright one,
the bright woman.
Your father and your brothers are all visible:
wrapped in the sun
they are the searching light of consciousness,
energy and action,
and true, the moon rises nightly above the street-lights,
but she is virginal,
so where are you, the dazzling goddess, the bold lover,
who sets the earth growing?

From this high window I can make out nothing.
I turn, find the stairs, descend.
In the centre of the house, waiting quietly,
you, my friend.
The daylight from the window is falling across you.
I see that you shine.

I think Inanna's light is not from the mind,
but from the heart-centre.
Perhaps it spurts like milk from her breasts,
and we, her children,
suck daylight as it streams white from her sky.

I walk to the window.
The city is held in the circle of the day.

Loss of Paradise

Why does Inanna descend?
She has no need.
She is queen of heaven,
she walks in Paradise,
and when she moves among the jewelled trees
animals and coloured birds
fan like a wave around her.

She is not banished.
She chooses.

Is it love that causes her to come down?
Does she feel pity for
the frenzy and sadness
of our consuming city,
and think that by taking her sister in her arms
she can transform her rage,
comfort, calm and heal her?

Or is that interpretation
too easy?

Why does the soul come down?
Why decide to enter
this maze of flesh,
and as a child, too:
a child may be utterly abandoned
and as it doesn't understand measure, its terror
has no boundaries?

Can she be hunting a centre?
Or danger even?

Or is Inanna's descent
more like when I chose to quarrel
with you, the friend I love?
All was as usual in our comfortable kitchen,
and reminiscent of Eden,
till I, suffocating, screamed those hurtful words
and broke out into the night.

Was I then like Inanna
falling freely?

The ways of the gods are inscrutable.
Even though the drama
is crowded into us
and we are the theatre,
they still work deviously behind the scenes,
only occasionally revealing
unexpected bits of story-line or set.

Job-like we are left to guess
their motives.

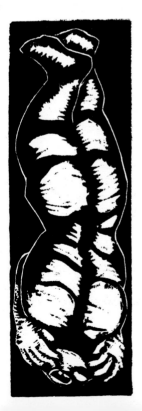

Inanna Descends

The coldest, darkest part of winter and, jaunty and well-prepared,
Inanna approaches the first gate of the underworld.

"I am Inanna, let me pass."
"You may pass if you hand over your briefcase."
"But I need it for my work"
"You have no right to question our perfect laws."

So Inanna surrenders her briefcase, and as the gate closes
behind her she knows there will be no more excited conferring
with colleagues, solving problems. She will never achieve
her ambitions or be praised for a job well done. She has been
dispensed with.
And so she comes to the second gate.

"I am Inanna, let me pass."
The guard goes through her pockets and takes her house keys.
"Are you stealing my house too?"
"You have no right to question our perfect laws."

So now Inanna has no home to return to at night. She has to
move continually from one lodging to another. She wanders
the city a stranger. All her friends are lost.
And so she comes to the third gate.

"I am Inanna, let me pass."
The guard grabs her hand and pulls off her ring.
"Don't do that!"
"What right have you to question our perfect laws?"

So now Inanna's relationship is over. There is no-one to be
concerned when she is ill, to joke or eat with, or to be
comfortable with or tender.
She comes to the fourth gate.

"I am Inanna, let me pass."
The guard snatches her handbag, takes out the photos of her
family and tears them up.

"No, not them - please, not them!"

But still her children whom she has loved so passionately, the
most precious part of her life, are taken from her, and she
is entirely alone.
And she comes to the fifth gate.

The guard plucks at her skirt. "All these pretty clothes - you
won't need them."
"Won't you leave me anything? Must I be completely naked?"
"You have no right to question."

So Inanna, who has so often made love with Dumuzi
with pleasure,
is forced to strip in front of the jeering guard.
And, naked and humiliated she comes to the sixth gate.

The guard drags at her hair. "I must have this now."
"That too?"
"You have no right."

So Inanna's head is shaved, and with her hair she loses her
strength and health.
And she drags herself, sick and hopeless, to the seventh gate.

"Now give me part of your flesh. Your womb or your breast
you must give."
Inanna has no strength to question.

And so the guard, following his perfect laws cuts away part
of her body.

And now, at last, she is ready to enter the presence of her sister,
Ereshkigal.

Ereshkigal Receives Inanna

Ereshkigal sees that her sister,
deprived of everything she valued,
still shines with a milky light,
and she is full of envy
and kicks Inanna to the floor
and cries out:

"Why have you come to meddle here
where I administer my perfect laws?
Do you imagine you can win me with love?
Why should I want your love
if you reject my anger?
Do you think you can bring me healing?
Why should I need your healing
when you despise my destroying?

Proudly you boast your sky of love
spreads over the earth
like a tent over refugees in the mountains.
I tell you, sister,
all the creatures who gorge on flesh
or eat decaying matter
crowd under my protection.
Yes, even your precious seeds, eggs, children
originate in my destruction.

Stand up before me!
Look into my eyes!
Remember those who grow towards your sky
see only death beyond them.
Stare deep into my eyes!
Your death is waiting!"

Death of Inanna

And now at last for Inanna
there is no more need for striving or
for ambition, for reconciling
the needs of others, finding an identity,
deciding.

Slipping quietly into her sister's lap,
she lies quite still.
As from sick-rooms and hospitals
all across the city
the dying, as I write,
are burrowing like children
into the wide lap of night.

And Ereshkigal?
Did she embrace her sister?
Is such enfolding an embrace?
Did she love her sister?
Can final hate be love?
When she fixed her with the eyes of death
were they also the eyes of birth?
Is complete destruction
also new beginning?

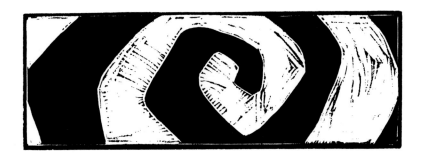

The Kurgarra and Galatur cry with Ereshkigal

Ereshkigal is crying out in pain
and the kurgarra and galatur are crying with her.
"Oh, oh," she moans,
and "Oh," they moan with her.
They don't try to comfort,
stifle or gloss over:
they cry with her.

Ereshkigal is roaring with anger,
and the kurgarra and galatur are beside her.
"Ah, ah" she growls,
and "Necessity," they say.
They don't urge reason
or call for forgiveness:
they listen.

For her it is like suddenly swimming,
like coming to an edge,
stepping over and floating.
And "Yes," she murmurs from the margin,
"Yes, you may have my sister's carcass."

Pondering the Kurgarra and the Galatur

Let us pause now to consider
the galatur and the kurgarra,
for it seems pertinent to ask
why they are suited for this task,
and what strange or crazy god would choose
to pick his fingernails and use
the muck beneath, and why he creates
two such unlikely candidates
to be the rescuers, the heroes
who buzz through cracks to interpose
between the sisters. It's odd, what's more,
that on these two, unknown before,
should hinge the whole crux of the story
when they are clearly unsuited for glory,
having no gender, looks nor frame,
nothing, it seems, beyond a name.

Perhaps the gods to tantalise
are dangling a gobbet of surprise,
or maybe this passage demonstrates
the theory of chaos - that which states
the flitting of a butterfly's wing
may multiply, expand and bring
gales and hurricanes. Perhaps in the heart
from a similar insignificant start
great change may follow: in a gathering flow
once static character traits may go,
fears may be lost, resentments shed,
Inanna may be raised from the dead.

Beads of Wisdom

Inanna lies splayed across the floor of death
and the kurgarra and galatur feed and sprinkle her
till breath begins chokingly as in a cold motor.
But just as life engages and she prepares to start moving,
she sees, as if dreaming, beads of wisdom
beside her on the floor. She claws them toward her,
straining fingers still stiff with death,
and secures them in her fist before life blocks her vision.

And when she stands up to stretch, the purple-black beads,
roll down her arms past muscles, bones, ligaments,
and, as marbles in a bagatelle lodge in different pockets,
they rock and settle in her body's separate chakras,
each bead caught up in its particular coil.

So when Inanna steps from death out towards her sister,
her quieter light leaves the blackness less blinding:
stalagmites stand fantastic, deep pools shine indigo,
rocks are decorated with moisture, crystals, precious stones,
now they are lit from a body starred, scarred with darkness,
studded at its centres with clusters of black experience.

Shape-shifters

When Ereshkigal spies her sister
she screams, "You are my food, my meat!
I shall chew up your glistening whiteness,
I intend to feast on you yet."

Inanna smiles and stretches,
she's a carefree, skittering hare,
and a hound baying behind her
is tearing her gleaming fur.

Inanna turns and wriggles,
all fins and gills, a fish,
and an otter diving on her
is slashing her milky flesh.

Inanna flips and sparkles,
a wave prinked, scalloped with foam,
and a seal surfing over her
is slurping her complex comb.

Till, tasted and relished, Inanna
becomes a buoyant, rising bird,
who, untangling from her snaky sister,
soars to the sky from the underworld.

But those filched beads of wisdom
keep niggling and complaining,
"The clouds are too white, the air's too pure,
this hovering is too straining."

Till at last Inanna, plummeting,
acknowledges she's incomplete
and cries, "Sister, climb to the surface,
there heaven and hell must meet."

Ereshkigal's Climb

Ereshkigal:
For you it's easy.
Your light feet, like Christ's,
always float above the painting,
But I'm at the bottom,
not an amazed disciple,
but like a rock
which can't soar up or hop,
pole-vault, prance, leap over -
no, not even heave
one sluggish, heavy foot
above the other.

Inanna:
In my mind's eye
I see two rivers,
one flows downhill,
one up, so close
that between them both
channels run easily.
I need you near me.
Besides you are no rock:
you're a frog with a brave spring,
a whale, a dolphin,
poised to fling out over the waves!

Ereshkigal:
Each step up this shaft a labour!
I muster strength,
struggle upward,
slip back.
My sack-like body,
sagging with seeds and eggs,
is astraddle a massive abyss.
I'm terrified I shall tumble,
nose-dive, crash down.
I can't climb higher!
Can't!

Inanna:
When I look down
I see a black fire below me,
a purple flame
closed in, hidden in stone.
Let it erupt now, roar out,
so you can dart up, sister, fight up,
fist up, pour up, shoot up,
burst out!

Ereshkigal:
I hang now below the surface,
where tree-roots, seaweed, fungi
shut me out like a valve.
I'm bone-tired, knackered,
I've toiled too hard.
I have no thrust left to push past
this last obstruction.

Inanna:
I am reaching down,
my arms make a channel.
Swim into this birth-canal, sister,
squirm, tumble up, be born,
blue, wet and squalling,
onto my breast.

Ereshkigal Comes to the Surface

Atoms, disordered, cause
blast and destruction,
and Ereshkigal compresses
the whole molten centre,
so when she gashes a passage
through the skin of the planet,
her terrible crowning
leaves the ground wounded.
She is like roaring oil
flaming suddenly skyward,
white water upgushing
in a tidal-wave fountain.
She ruptures the rivers
she nudges the mountains,
her fearsome birthing
leaves life's intertwining
torn out and broken,
bleeding and changing.

The Meeting

Inanna's arms,
outstretched like a net,
gather the force-shoal that spreads
ahead of Ereshkigal,
but her sister's whale-fury
is too enormous:
it unbalances her and,
because she won't leave hold,
the two go spinning.

They roll over like children -
the sky coming and going,
and the ground coming and going.

A fat dandelion head blowing,
or two clowns cartwheeling,
they tumble across the surface
unreeling creeper streamers,
peppering beetles,
blowing out coloured trees,
spluttering water-spouts.

And as they go they shout:
"We two are one
and lots and mixtured,
not black or white but multi-coloured.
Watch our drum turning,
flecked with soap,
see strawberry love,
jet-pain, green-shoot anger,
ice-cream laughter splattering,
every jiffy a different pattern."

Then with a contrary current,
they pause, hover,
and bounce gently back
across their new-laid world,
spiky now with tendrils,
and they pluck bits out,
and wind bits in again,
and sing:

"We are quietness, too,
friendship, tenderness
and sleep.
Our day-night arms
hold everything.
Pour in your mistakes,
your hatred or stupidity,
we two conjurors
will scrub, rinse, bleach,
kiss, cuddle, caress,
till - hey presto! -
you can pull them out
fluttering."

A Prayer

Fill me with your love, Inanna.
Give me your different vision.
Stretch out across my sky.
Be clear to me as to the desert-dwellers.
And be strong,
firm to catch the sister who emerges
and hold her spiralling.

And Ereshkigal,
you with your meat-hook in your hand,
keeper of the centre,
we need you.
We will turn to you –
and if we turn
divert your anger from us,
let your force be transformed,
circle mildly in your sister's arms,
spare us catastrophe, dark goddess.

All across the city now,
up from below concrete,
blossom is pouring.
Be like the blossom, Ereshkigal.
Come up as spring.
As spring,
        after spring,
                after spring.

Other poems

Something New on the Island

There stands on the island, bare on the skyline,
and I wait on the shore.
It was some words you spoke, now forgotten,
which caused me to come here,
and though I can't recall what you were saying,
I'm excited, I'm expecting change,
looking to a dawn miracle,
and already the sky is greying.

Perhaps grass will sprout from those rocks
and a tree unfurl in the centre,
or it could be I shall see a romance,
a bed will be laid for a marriage,
and Inanna will come with her lover,
or Isis will lie with her brother
in a union to bless and stir the earth below,
cause fruit to form, seedlings to grow.

But as I don't remember what you said,
and, as I stand here on the shore,
I don't yet know what I'll witness
when the sun comes up and it's dawn.
It could be a different celebration –
the return of the prodigal from the wild,
a birth or a raising from the dead,
or the plucking from the sea of a child.

* * * * * * *

When it came it was quite unexpected –
it was a landing of angels! –
two of them arriving with the light.
They came from far in the huge sky,
and at first I thought them meteorites,
then eagles, till they suddenly tumbled,
wings flapping, like peewits
practising their aerobatic flight.

They plunged down close past me,
and I saw, astonished, that their bodies
weren't solid, but made of moving parts –
feathers, seeds, stars, drops of dew
and rainbows, suitable for angels,
as well as particles of dung and compost,
sawdust, maggots, bits of waste-matter,
which, moving, were suitable too.

They landed gawkily and stood still,
looking back on the sun they had come from,
their wings outstretched like cormorants',
while the island, a sea monster,
held her breath, waiting the unknown,
They preened themselves, she trembled
and her fringe-waves roared a greeting
as they began to step across her stones.

That was when you called me and I left.
I don't know, but I guess that later
the angels shot off particles
as catherine-wheels whirl off sparks
(perhaps they cart-wheeled and danced)
and those fragments of dung and seed and feathers
were what started the new species
which are surely now growing on the island.

Ships

Now that I have embarked on this new vessel,
I want to look back on some of my other ships —
the liner, for instance, where the pounding of the engine
was louder than the sound of the tide and the ocean,
and where we thought the messages of the passengers
disputing around bars and through dance-music,
more important than the speaking of the water.
We knew there were icebergs, but we were protected by steel.

After the steam-ship came a sailing vessel
whose sounds were different: her rigging and decking
her masts and her sails all moved in unison
with the moods of the ocean. We heard the sea's voice then,
but only as foreign speech, for we were passers-by,
our purposeful passage cut through her crests and tides,
our minds were brooding on our merchandise,
we ploughed her, we used her, pushed her endlessly aside.

But now that I am drifting in the curragh
I know that there are milder ways of touching water.
This boat's skins and timbers flex with the swell,
she is like a great fish swimming with the current,
and in a curragh, in the wake of the saints,
you can throw away the oars, put up the awning,
let the sea direct your journey and pick your landing,
while you listen to her myths and music, her unfathomable calling.

And now as I am drifting and dreaming about my past,
I remember the liner was not the first vessel.
Far before that comes a perpetual rocking motion,
while by my ears the pulse murmurs and surges ......
am I lying in my moses-basket, my boat of rushes?
Nor will this barque, this curragh, be my last,
for now I've heard the hugeness of the ocean,
the unexpected booming of her waters beyond the sea,
I want each boat to bring me closer to her,
till I'm back in my crib of rushes, or in the whales belly,
or floating on foam or seaweed unravelled by the waves.

White for You

Though the snow that matched you, my dear, is gone,
you are still white to me;
as white, you seem, as the doves' wings
catching the light as they rise in a flutter
into the squally sky,
as white as the hedges of the blackthorn blossom,
or the extravagant canopy
which heaves and tumbles on my neighbour's tree
across the storm-purple and grey.
Where is my purple, you say, where is my black?
They are the backdrop, let them be.

I see you in all the glistening and gleaming
between the April rains,
your shine is in the silver of pussy-willow,
though not in the catkins, they are too yellow
and the brilliant leaf-greens
are too earthy, I take them for me;
but the purples and blacks –
true, sometime I must reach out and use them,
maybe even clothe you in them,
but between us at this time,
in this spring I thought I might not see,
let them be, let them be.

Beginning Again

You did not make me, God out of dead clay:
I was already with you on that day,
nor was the clay dead, it was live earth
which circled into flesh.
I was then like Sophia, I was like Eve
the mother of all living things,
and from my belly, from my generous thighs
poured out bees, moths, wasps, beetles and lice,
all kinds of squawkers, scuttlers, hummers, swoopers -
creatures galore. I cradled them,
I nourished them with my milk, or, changing form,
became a child and played with them,
a foundling, who Remus-like fed from their teats
so they were part of me.
My breath was then the constant-watching doe,
my heart the quiet-eyed ox,
lions and tigers stalked my forest-guts
and round and round my spine curled up the snakes.
And, as now through the floor of a deserted house,
grass then grew massed and tangled through my veins,
blood and sap ran together, roots round my bones,
and all my skin tingling and itching with flowers.

After the flowers, the fruit,
and then came the Fall - was there a Fall?
Or was there just a turning of the head
so what is joined seemed single, separate
If I were now to shift and change position,
could I feel flowers pricking through my skin?
Could I expand, become springy, earthy, huge,
tunnelled by voles and foxes, soaked by storms,
crammed full of seed and larvae? Could I again
feed, cradle all my creatures, watch them play,
and all would be as it were on that first day?

Fish Lady: Shape-shifter

"This fish", she murmurs as she slits
and slices it into portions, "sucked flavour
from coconut beaches and tundra lakes,
took texture from froth edges
and black, unmoving bottom water.
Such a world-crammed dish, sir, will surely satisfy
your wide-splashed appetite!"

She digs out umber and purple guts,
lines them beside already hacked-off heads,
wraps the body and hands him the dead-weight.
"A lovely mackerel for eighty pence."
Haddock-yellow, salmon-pink, dab-brown,
gills, frills and edge-stitched fillets embroider
the slab she leans across.

Her necklace is of crabs, her earrings shrimps.
Scallops adorn the hemline of a dress
part see-through, part speckled silver.
The filmy fabric washes round his limbs
along with seaweed, fins and foam, in the cave
where beautiful, patient, inscrutable,
she sits enthroned.

Till he wriggles up into her mouth,
and thumbs down her gullet to await the time,
when she, her world-swim over, will be served
at the king's table, and when,
after the slitting of the underbelly,
he can put aside the flesh again
and step out, ready.

Old Woman and Clouds

An old woman now,
I have lived for too long on the edge of the caravan park.
The shop has closed down,
and the caravans nearest mine are deserted.
I rarely go out.
Usually I sit and listen to the sea
and the wind playing through the old metal and the park's pines,
and I watch white, green and purple clouds as they
crumple and uncrumple
over the cliff edge.

But yesterday I walked out through the park
and passed people round a bonfire.
They are all strangers now,
but they called me back and I sat with them.
I drank with them,
and, while the crowd clapped and cheered,
what possessed me? – I danced with one!

Later a child, staring, asked:
"Why does she keep opening and shutting her mouth, Mum?"
– a tiny child's question,
and I heard the young woman her mother reply:
"Hush, Tina, she's an old lady talking to the gods."
What an imagination!
As I look out over the cliffs I am smiling still –
"Talking to the gods!"

Black Fox

We had never seen the black fox so plainly,
though certainly we knew she was around –
had found corpses, noticed rubbish disturbed,
heard howls in the dark mornings,
and, like Aborigine women at the bull-roarers,
the two of us, so unguarded, had cowered.

But that day we saw her in full sunlight,
uncamouflaged. We came round the house
and she was crouched, menacing, waiting for us.
I thought of the night sky – its louring dark
and leaping planets. I thought of chaos
poised to unlock itself in hurtling stars.

So frail you were then, I moved to protect you,
and with my movement she was lost –
gone back to earth, perhaps, I couldn't tell,
only I marvel that I saw her so close,
for, though I've heard her I have not seen her since,
nor understood what it is she wants of us.

Come out, black fox, let me judge your pitch,
measure your teeth and muscles, gauge your spring.
For now I could arm myself with knife and axe,
ambush and savage you, hack your massive neck,
slit open your belly and pare your sparkling fur,
and we should not again hear your wild howls and cower.

But would there be others then? Should I not kill
but follow you, black fox, learn your call,
pull on your skin of shadows? Or maybe lure you,
tame you, train you like a dog and fondle you?
If I were to take you in my arms and kiss you,
would you, black fox, like the beast, be transformed?

Breastplate

Should I wear it into his presence –
this jangling Brunhilde breastplate?
It would mean I'd have to ignore
the sniggerers and the workmen
leaning out from the scaffolding,
but I should find it really satisfying
to burst in through his door,
and prance around, and dazzle him
with silver disks and glitter
and pink shimmering baubles,
and shout, "Oh no, don't jeer!
If it seems to you like a piece of theatre,
that's because it's made from signifiers
outside your single sphere.
It was not made by machine, either,
not even by hand, but by arms, rather,
that encircled me, leaving an imprint
of links and disks, and the colours rose
out of my centre, through the skin.
So don't dare gloat over your skill!
Though I stand with one breast mutilated
and now the other is awaiting it,
however sharp you've honed your steel,
your scythe won't cut through this!
Look, this is my amazing breastplate
that heals and makes all things well."

Two into Three won't go

There are three people in the room -
you, me, and the stag.
The stag's meaning is in his antlers and knees.
His legs are expressive.
His backbone flies at a tangent.
He divides the space geometrically.

I am trying to solve the mathematics,
or at least lay out the problem his presence sets
Not understanding, I make wild guesses:
The rutting season? Abbots Bromley
A phallic symbol or a personal hurt?
Bambi? A hart by the stream panting?

The figure, however, is complex.
Even if I knew what I was trying to prove,
there is no obvious square or hypotenuse,
and, since alive, he keeps shaking his head
or shifting his weight so digits on the hock
drop to the hoof and all the angles change.

But you're there, peaceful on his other side,
so expound to me the theorem that will make it easy,
or help me freeze him till I get it right!
What? Not the same answer? I don't believe it!
How can your side have different matrices?
How can a stag be assymetrical?

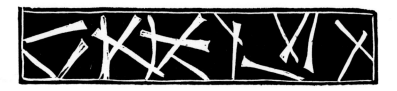

For my Grandchild

For your coming
I am knitting a jacket and bootees,
looping coloured wools into flowers and leaves,
and I was going to say
that while I weave wool
your mother, my daughter, is weaving flesh for you.
But no,
Surely, even now,
tiny, unformed as you are,
you are knitting yourself into being.
She, the great provider, is pulling out yarns
for you to choose from,
but already your little fingers are knotting together
your own intricate and special pattern.

So what should a grandmother's prayer for you be?
I pray that as you grow up
and start to pick out strands from the world's stock,
its range of colours won't be too depleted –
there'll still be shades and textures of every kind
for you to draw into your fabric.
I do not ask that the dull hues or blacks
should pass you by.
No. I want you to make use of the whole spectrum of colours
and call on such imagination
as will create a splendid and fabulous pattern,
far more daring than these little flowers
I am engaged on.